POSSI
BILIT
OLOGY

POSSI BILIT OLOGY

IT'S A GREAT DAY TO BE AMAZING

VALLORI THOMAS

Published by
Mynd Matters Publishing
715 Peachtree Street NE, Suites 100 & 200
Atlanta, GA 30308
www.myndmatterspublishing.com

978-1-948145-32-9 (pbk)
978-1-948145-34-3 (ebk)

FIRST EDITION

COVER DESIGN BY DEMARCUS MCGAUGHEY

To Grandma:
Even now at age 100, you are my tireless
CHAMPION, the one who has always been my
rock and the opening to grace and possibility. I
am proud to dedicate this triumphant book to
you, who taught me to prevail again and again.

To Mom:
You are my loving and beautiful connection to a
long line of exceptional women. In dedicating
this book to you, I honor your tenacity
and resilience.

CONTENTS

PREFACE

*I*t is never too late to have a happy life.

That simple concept rests at the center of a life perspective I call, ***Possibilitology.***

There was a time when I couldn't see possibility of any kind. I had lost everything including my home, my job, my family, and my friends. Along with everything else went any respect I had for myself. Looking back, the only thing that rivaled my loss of self-respect was the loss of respect I once had for other human beings.

Without self-esteem and self-respect, I didn't have a glimmer of hope.

I hit bottom and it was far lower and emptier than I ever imagined it could be. When you can't see possibility of any kind, not only do you not know how high you can fly, you don't know how deep you can sink.

Frankly, the depth of the human spirit is unfathomable. A person has to plummet a great distance spiritually before she hits bottom and you don't know where the bottom is until you hit it. That's what happened to me. I found my bottom to be a cold, isolated, and lonely place. Although I felt it wasn't a place where I could stay and still be alive, I lingered there anyway. Hopeless. Indecisive. Directionless.

Over time, I came to realize the impact and degree of

my isolation and detachment. There are extended periods in my past of which I have no memory. While most people celebrate holidays with family and have pictures and stories to share, for me, many years that should be filled with those types of memories are instead replaced with gaps and emptiness. Pictures with family and friends that should trigger memories don't exist. There are huge swaths of my past from which there is no one to say, remember the time we did this or that.

I wish I could tell you exactly what happened to spark my life's turnaround but I can't. I do not know if it was something someone said to me, something I read on a billboard, or something my inner voice whispered. I only know there came a divine moment when I knew the direction I should move was up—up from my bottom.

Slowly, piece by piece, I began to rebuild my life. The spiritual void within me was so great though, I could only measure my growth in things like wearing clean clothes that fit, sleeping in the same bed under the same roof every night, and looking people in the eye and speaking to them without hurling razor-sharp expletives.

One day after being unemployable for God only knows how long, I found a job and for the first time in a long time, I embraced the opportunity to develop substantive relationships. I finally reconnected with humanity.

The only way for human beings to experience themselves as being human is in relationship with other human beings.

I soon discovered I was pretty good at being human. (Who knew?) People seemed to enjoy being around me and one day during an ordinary conversation with coworkers about nothing in particular, a colleague asked, "What do you really want?"

I was stupefied and couldn't answer. *What do I want?*

I can only imagine what I must have looked like to my coworkers in that moment when, as the resident "Chatty Kathy," I couldn't find one thing to say. It was a simple enough question and yet, it was so potent it stopped me in my tracks. *What do I want?*

Years later, in the methodical rebuilding of my life, I would come to understand how pivotal that question was and how it set me on the path to the life perspective at the center of who I am and everything I do. ***Possibilitology*** is a perspective that can make every day amazing.

What Is *Possibilitology*?

It begins with possibility thinking (PT), a mindset that engages in the exploration of possibility. It allows you to engage in transforming what is, into what might be. When my coworker asked her seemingly innocuous question, it triggered my possibility thinking. What stunned me was the realization of how vast the possibilities were in response to the question.

Little to no creativity can occur without possibility thinking. PT forces you to ask solution-oriented questions and requires you to form your own creative responses which leads to a sense of self-determination. Self-determination is essential for taking intentional actions and for being imaginative and innovative.

With PT as the foundation, *Possibilitology* rests on the three pillars of amazingness: Centering, Expansion, and Emergence.

Centering: It is the alignment of the spiritual and physical aspects of who you are. It is a state of being, of being present and/or having awareness in every moment. Centering creates balance and stability in our physical and our emotional state and brings acceptance that we are here to fulfill a purpose. It brings strength that allows for expansion and emergence. By the time I hit bottom, none of this was available to me. I certainly didn't have a sense of purpose and my cognitive, physical, and emotional states existed not in balance, but in the extreme.

Expansion: Imagine a box filled with everything you know and have known, everything you do and have done, and everything you are and have been. There's only so much that the box can hold, right? Well, expansion means creating a bigger box.

In my case, I lived on the margins of society. My "box" had shrunk so dramatically that my life was barely recognizable as life itself.

Emergence: This usually occurs at the intersection of danger and opportunity. Sometimes the difference between danger and opportunity is simply how you look at a situation. Emergence is choosing to move forward or upward and results in increased zest for life and a more rewarding life strategy.

What follows is a primer in *Possibilitology,* a life perspective aimed at having every day be amazing for you and the people around you. Each chapter is divided into seven days of targeted insights, which allows you to spend the whole week on that perspective. Read the chapter. Take notes. Ponder the information. Journal about your insights and inspirations. Embody each "Amazing Day Maker."

While some weeks will focus on Centering, others will delve into Expansion or Emergence. At the end of twelve weeks, you will have a working understanding of the *Possibilitology* perspective and a personal, self-generated handbook for how to apply it in your life.

Today is a great day to be amazing! Let's get started.

CENTERING

The alignment of the spiritual and the physical aspects of who you are.

THE JOURNEY BEGINS WITH *I AM*

"*We* are not human beings having a spiritual experience. We are spiritual beings having a human experience." These are the words of Pierre Teilhard de Chardin, the French philosopher and Jesuit priest whose theological teachings were recently cited by Pope Francis.

Whether this is your first time hearing it or you've heard it before, there is probably something about this idea that resonates for you. Did you experience yourself nodding in agreement or having an "ah-ha" moment? The Universe is always speaking to us in one way or another and I'm going to assert that if the philosopher's statement resonated with you, it was because you were listening to the Universe, not me.

There is something deep inside every human being, sometimes at a subconscious level, that senses we are somehow more than just physical beings and are not defined by time and circumstance. We are born knowing innately of our untethered spiritual nature. Add to it life's conditioning and circumstances and we soon drift away from the essence of who we are. We become a compacted blend of what we do, where we live, who we associate with, our successes and failures, and our opinions and outlooks.

Centering brings us back to the original and authentic self—the spiritual self. In doing so, we are better able to be present or to be in the present from moment to moment to moment.

As more will be uncovered as we continue on this journey, let's begin to focus on the first step in your Centering practice, I AM.

I AM is the metaphysical name of the spiritual self, as distinguished from the human self. One is governed by Spirit and the other is led by personal will, time, and circumstance. I AM is eternal, without beginning or ending because I AM exists in every moment. When you allow yourself to be fully present or fully in the present, it starts with a declaration of I AM.

The Universe, often referred to as God, Buddha, Allah, or Jehovah, among others, is always working and abiding on your behalf. Declaring I AM is the gateway to what the Universe holds for you. So, when you declare I AM, be specific and intentional because what follows "I AM" will bring either success or failure.

You can't escape being you, so declare yourself as I AM powerfully in a way that creates the you that you'd never want to escape.

AMAZING DAY-MAKER 1: I AM

_____

_____

_____

Pillar One
MY AMAZING DAY-MAKER JOURNAL

Day 1: What follows I AM can determine the kind of life you live. It's an awesome power that can send you into despair (I am lonely) or exhilaration (I am blessed). Fill this page with I AM statements that lift you up.

_____

_____

_____

_____

_____

_____

_____

_____

_____

_____

_____

_____

_____

_____

_____

_____

<u>Pillar One</u>
MY AMAZING DAY-MAKER JOURNAL

Day 2: Joel Osteen, an American author and televangelist, says, "Whatever you follow "I AM" with, you're handing it an invitation, opening the door, and giving it permission to be in your life." What are you opening the door to? What new invitations are you sending out to empower your life?

_____

_____

_____

_____

_____

_____

_____

_____

_____

_____

_____

_____

Pillar One

MY AMAZING DAY-MAKER JOURNAL

Day 3: If you haven't said it already, do you dare say, "I am beautiful. I am attractive?" And if you have said it already, do you dare expound upon it as the self-image that you're taking forward into the future? Beauty is in being confident about who God made you to be. Fill this page with I AM statements that reinforce how beautiful you are.

_____

_____

_____

_____

_____

_____

_____

_____

_____

_____

_____

_____

_____

Pillar One
MY AMAZING DAY-MAKER JOURNAL

Day 4: You have something to offer the world that is unique. What is it? What's great about you?

_____

_____

_____

_____

_____

_____

_____

_____

_____

_____

_____

_____

_____

_____

_____

_____

Pillar One
MY AMAZING DAY-MAKER JOURNAL

Day 5: What does it mean to be the queen or king of your life?

_____

_____

_____

_____

_____

_____

_____

_____

_____

_____

_____

_____

_____

_____

_____

_____

<u>Pillar One</u>

MY AMAZING DAY-MAKER JOURNAL

Day 6: You are an amazing day maker. How do you feel about that declaration?

_____

_____

_____

_____

_____

_____

_____

_____

_____

_____

_____

_____

_____

_____

_____

Pillar One
MY AMAZING DAY-MAKER JOURNAL

Day 7: Complete this statement: I am looking forward to and encouraged by the future because:

_____

_____

_____

_____

_____

_____

_____

_____

_____

_____

_____

_____

_____

_____

_____

_____

_____

COMPARISON CAN STEAL YOUR JOY

*E*xperts say measuring yourself against others is something the human mind is predisposed to doing. It's normal to wonder how we measure up to other people. According to social comparison theory, this drive is part of our basic desire to understand ourselves and our place in the social world. But dwelling too much on these judgments has a cost and the impact of such comparison can be a boost or a burden.

It is possible to compare your achievements to someone else's and feel motivated to improve your own life. And recognizing that your abilities may be a notch or two above someone else's can be like a B-12 shot to your self-esteem. But comparison can be harmful when it leaves you feeling inferior or depressed. It's harmful when it robs you of joy and a sense of fulfillment.

Psychologists divide social comparisons into two main categories, downward and upward. Downward comparison involves comparing yourself to someone you perceive as worse off than yourself, while upward comparison involves comparing yourself to someone you perceive as better off. The comparisons may be based on appearance, achievement, health, intelligence, ability, social status, wealth, or any other attribute.

Research suggests we are more likely to make

downward comparisons when our self-esteem is threatened (for example, if we've recently received negative feedback) because these comparisons give us a boost, enhance our own perceived standing, and reassure us that things could be worse.

Upward comparison, on one hand, can boost self-esteem by providing inspiration and hope, motivating us to improve our own situation, and providing useful information about how to overcome an obstacle. It can also boost self-esteem such as when we bask in the reflected glory of a successful close friend or family member.

On the other hand, upward comparison can fuel envy and low self-esteem because it can overlook the complexity of other people's lives or even our own. So, what's the key to using comparison effectively? Perspective. Choose the right perspective when making comparisons.

Since comparison is a fundamental human impulse, like breathing, you can't turn it off. But if you understand its origins and know what to watch out for, you can overcome the adverse effects of comparison and amplify the good effects. So, let's amend my earlier statement. Comparison can rob you of joy and a sense of fulfillment, if you allow it.

But what do you do when comparison begins to take up too much space in your head? I'll tell you what my mentor said when I was letting comparison get the best of me. She said, "**STOP IT!**" That's right, stop it!

It tickles me every time I think about it. But those two words remain some of the most potent coaching I've ever received. Two simple words that give pause, create freedom, and allow for a mental and spiritual reset.

AMAZING DAY MAKER 2: Stop it! If the grass looks greener on the other side, maybe you should focus on your own lawn.

<u>Pillar One</u>

MY AMAZING DAY-MAKER JOURNAL

Day 8: What are your beliefs about comparison? How have your beliefs about comparison shaped your life?

_____

_____

_____

_____

_____

_____

_____

_____

_____

_____

_____

_____

_____

_____

_____

<u>Pillar One</u>
MY AMAZING DAY-MAKER JOURNAL

Day 9: Think of a well-known person, living or historical, whom you admire. What do you admire about them? Why?

_____

_____

_____

_____

_____

_____

_____

_____

_____

_____

_____

_____

_____

_____

_____

_____

Pillar One
MY AMAZING DAY-MAKER JOURNAL

Day 10: Today, I'd like you to think of a person whom you admire, living or historical, who is not well-known. Perhaps the person is your family member, colleague, spiritual advisor, teacher, or friend. What do you admire about them? Why?

_____

_____

_____

_____

_____

_____

_____

_____

_____

_____

_____

_____

_____

_____

_____

<u>Pillar One</u>

MY AMAZING DAY-MAKER JOURNAL

Day 11: Now think about yourself and write down the things people have said that they admire in you or that you know people would admire in you if they knew about it.

_____

_____

_____

_____

_____

_____

_____

_____

_____

_____

_____

_____

_____

_____

Pillar One

MY AMAZING DAY-MAKER JOURNAL

Day 12: Review what you wrote on Days 9, 10, and 11. Circle all of the attributes that the three people have in common. Write them here and begin with I AM:

_____

_____

_____

_____

_____

_____

_____

_____

_____

_____

_____

_____

_____

_____

<u>Pillar One</u>
MY AMAZING DAY-MAKER JOURNAL

Day 13: You are an amazing day maker. How do you feel about that?

_____

_____

_____

_____

_____

_____

_____

_____

_____

_____

_____

_____

_____

_____

_____

_____

Pillar One

MY AMAZING DAY-MAKER JOURNAL

Day 14: Complete the following statement, being as descriptive as possible: I am looking forward to and encouraged by the future because:

_____

_____

_____

_____

_____

_____

_____

_____

_____

_____

_____

_____

_____

_____

_____

EVERYTHING THAT IS, WAS ONCE A THOUGHT

*E*verything that exists began as someone's thought. Whether you call it inner speech, self-talk, internal dialogue, or thinking to yourself, it has proven to be an important part of everyday life. Since thoughts become things, be careful about what you think.

Any conversation about Centering would be incomplete if we didn't address the "inner voice," especially the "inner critic," which some experts refer to as the "anti-self." One aspect of the inner voice speaks to us in a positive, life-affirming tone that represents our real self with authentic wants, desires, and goals. The other aspect, the inner critic, speaks in a harsh destructive tone. It is a nasty naysayer that can lead brilliant, creative minds (like yours) to ignore their dreams and undermine their goals.

I have been stalked by my inner critic far more than I care to admit. She has tried to thwart or minimize my dreams and goals like writing this book, creating workshops and product offerings, finding romance, and building wealth.

Getting to know and challenge your inner critic is an essential step in Centering, and in the quest to lead your best life. So how can you tap into your inner voice to engage the positive while quieting the inner critic? Be present. Listen. Connect. Be an observer of your thoughts. Give time and attention to the thoughts that nourish and empower your goals. Dismiss those that don't. These deliberate actions helped give me direction when it seemed like I had nowhere to go.

AMAZING DAY MAKER 3: Quiet the voice that says you can't. Cheer for the voice that says you can.

Pillar One

MY AMAZING DAY-MAKER JOURNAL

Day 15: What have you heard from self and others that weighs you down? What messages have said, "You can't?" Who communicates them to you most effectively? Your answers to these questions will be helpful in getting to know the voices that need to be quieted.

_____

_____

_____

_____

_____

_____

_____

_____

_____

_____

_____

_____

_____

_____

Pillar One
MY AMAZING DAY-MAKER JOURNAL

Day 16: Expose the naysayer. Self-talk can be subtle. What aspects of your greatness are you pretending not to know exist?

_____

_____

_____

_____

_____

_____

_____

_____

_____

_____

_____

_____

_____

_____

Pillar One
MY AMAZING DAY-MAKER JOURNAL

Day 17: What motivates you? Think of a time when someone said something to you that stirred your spirit into action. What did they say and what did it mean to you for them to say it?

_____

_____

_____

_____

_____

_____

_____

_____

_____

_____

_____

_____

_____

_____

Pillar One

MY AMAZING DAY-MAKER JOURNAL

Day 18: What achievements are you proudest of? What do those achievements say about you?

_____

_____

_____

_____

_____

_____

_____

_____

_____

_____

_____

_____

_____

_____

_____

_____

_____

Pillar One
MY AMAZING DAY-MAKER JOURNAL

Day 19: Review what you wrote on Days 16, 17, and 18. Circle the words or phrases that stand out or speak to you in some way. Using those words and phrases, write a statement, perhaps even a mantra, that you'll use whenever you need to quiet the voice that says, "You can't."

_____

_____

_____

_____

_____

_____

_____

_____

_____

_____

_____

_____

_____

Pillar One
MY AMAZING DAY-MAKER JOURNAL

Day 20: You are an amazing day maker. How do you feel about that?

_____

_____

_____

_____

_____

_____

_____

_____

_____

_____

_____

_____

_____

_____

Pillar One
MY AMAZING DAY-MAKER JOURNAL

Day 21: Complete this statement and be as detailed as you choose. I am looking forward to and encouraged by the future because:

_____

_____

_____

_____

_____

_____

_____

_____

_____

_____

_____

_____

_____

_____

_____

_____

EXPANSION

Creating a bigger box.

DO SOMETHING.

*M*aria Popova, the Bulgarian-born writer, blogger, and literary and cultural critic who now makes her home in Brooklyn, New York, said, "The ability to connect the seemingly unconnected and to meld existing knowledge into new insight about some element of how the world works, that's practical creativity. Then there's moral creativity, (which is applying) that skill towards some kind of wisdom on how the world ought to work."

This is at the heart of the Expansion Principle. The "box" that I mentioned earlier, the one filled with everything you know and have known, everything you do and have done, and everything you are and have been, will get bigger when you begin to reshape your existing knowledge into new insights. The box will get bigger when you get creative because a bigger box is essential to go from where you are to where you want to be.

When it comes to Expansion, timing tends to be the biggest issue for some. They wonder, Am I ready? Is this the right time? Am I too old? Are all of my "ducks in a row?" Am I too young?

But know this, you will never have enough evidence to indicate that it's the right time to act on manifesting your vision. No matter what the indicators are for you, there will always be another piece of evidence that you're waiting on or searching for. By the same token, you'll never have enough evidence to indicate that it's NOT the right time to act on manifesting your vision.

What's the solution then?

Every journey begins with the first step. This is my interpretation of the sixth-century BC philosopher, Lao Tzu's, well-known quote, *The journey of a thousand miles begins with one step.*

Even a mundane action like getting a drink of water from the kitchen faucet requires you to walk to the kitchen, get a glass, put it under the tap, turn on the water, and let the water flow into the glass before drinking it. I would argue that if taking the first step is essential for such a simple act as this, it is also necessary in achieving any goal. Take the FIRST step and the other steps will follow. Start to see your delay tactics in a different light and re-examine your values.

AMAZING DAY MAKER 4: Do something! An idea that isn't acted on will remain in the past forever. An intention that isn't formed can never be met. Do something now.

Pillar Two

MY AMAZING DAY-MAKER JOURNAL

Day 22: What are your values? What are the core beliefs that influence how you live your life?

_____

_____

_____

_____

_____

_____

_____

_____

_____

_____

_____

_____

_____

_____

_____

_____

Pillar Two
MY AMAZING DAY-MAKER JOURNAL

Day 23: What are some core values that you aspire to?

_____

_____

_____

_____

_____

_____

_____

_____

_____

_____

_____

_____

_____

_____

_____

_____

_____

Pillar Two
MY AMAZING DAY-MAKER JOURNAL

Day 24: Are your values and actions aligned? Have your actions compromised your values? Have your values impeded your actions?

_____

_____

_____

_____

_____

_____

_____

_____

_____

_____

_____

_____

_____

_____

_____

Pillar Two
MY AMAZING DAY-MAKER JOURNAL

Day 25: What results do you believe are most important for you to experience fulfillment?

_____

_____

_____

_____

_____

_____

_____

_____

_____

_____

_____

_____

_____

_____

Pillar Two
MY AMAZING DAY-MAKER JOURNAL

Day 26: Review what you wrote on Days 22, 23, 24, and 25. Circle the words or phrases that stand out or speak to you in some way. Using those words and phrases, write your new value statement.

_____

_____

_____

_____

_____

_____

_____

_____

_____

_____

_____

_____

_____

_____

_____

Pillar Two
MY AMAZING DAY-MAKER JOURNAL

Day 27: You are an amazing day maker. What value for yourself do you find in being that way?

_____

_____

_____

_____

_____

_____

_____

_____

_____

_____

_____

_____

_____

_____

_____

_____

<u>Pillar Two</u>

MY AMAZING DAY-MAKER JOURNAL

Day 28: Complete the following statement using as much detail as you see fit: I am eager to see what's next because:

_____

_____

_____

_____

_____

_____

_____

_____

_____

_____

_____

_____

_____

_____

_____

_____

DON'T BE "FUELED" BY FAKES

*W*hat if passion is the human equivalent of the fuel that powers your car? What if passion is the source that adds energy to your goals, dreams, and vision? What if passion is the spark that ignites living an inspired life? You'd be passionate right?

Well, that's exactly what passion is. It's what drives purposeful action. Passion is the gale force experience that intertwines your vision, values, and authenticity. With it, you can turn stumbling blocks into stepping stones. Without it, disappointment and frustration will weigh you down.

I tend to be an outwardly passionate person. People rarely have to ask me to speak up and I like gesturing with my hands when I speak. My friends would say that I am never at a loss for enthusiasm. But passion isn't how loud you speak. It's how loud your speaking is heard. The point is to move and inspire others, and thereby live an inspired life yourself. Your passion will be unmistakable, no matter how it is expressed.

> *"Every great dream begins with a dreamer. You have within you the strength, the patience, and the passion to reach for the stars to change the world."*
> – Harriet Tubman

AMAZING DAY MAKER 5: Focus on what excites you!

Pillar Two
MY AMAZING DAY-MAKER JOURNAL

Day 29: In your brain, neurons are firing, your amygdala is being triggered, dopamine is being released, and frontal lobe activity is being stimulated. But only you can describe what excitement is for you. What is excitement? What is exciting?

_____

_____

_____

_____

_____

_____

_____

_____

_____

_____

_____

_____

_____

_____

Pillar Two
MY AMAZING DAY-MAKER JOURNAL

Day 30: What's the spirit of achievement for you? How does the world know when you're jazzed about something you're doing?

_____

_____

_____

_____

_____

_____

_____

_____

_____

_____

_____

_____

_____

_____

Pillar Two
MY AMAZING DAY-MAKER JOURNAL

Day 31: Think of someone whose passion is a model for you. What is it about them and their passion that you aspire to?

_____

_____

_____

_____

_____

_____

_____

_____

_____

_____

_____

_____

_____

_____

Pillar Two
MY AMAZING DAY-MAKER JOURNAL

Day 32: Using the following quote by Maya Angelou as the basis for your answer, what would you say about your mission?

> *"My mission in life is not merely to survive, but to thrive; and to do so with some passion, some compassion, some humor, and some style."*

_____

_____

_____

_____

_____

_____

_____

_____

_____

_____

_____

_____

Pillar Two

MY AMAZING DAY-MAKER JOURNAL

Day 33: Do you know the words to *Hakuna Matata*, the song from Disney's, *The Lion King?* Write them and sing them out loud for as long as they make you happy. (Note: if you don't know the song, find it, listen to it, and learn the words.)

_____

_____

_____

_____

_____

_____

_____

_____

_____

_____

_____

_____

_____

_____

Pillar Two
MY AMAZING DAY-MAKER JOURNAL

Day 34: You are an amazing day maker. What value is there for you in being that way?

_____

_____

_____

_____

_____

_____

_____

_____

_____

_____

_____

_____

_____

<u>Pillar Two</u>

MY AMAZING DAY-MAKER JOURNAL

Day 35: Complete the following statement.

I am so eager to see what's next in my life that I cannot contain my:

_____

_____

_____

_____

_____

_____

_____

_____

_____

_____

_____

_____

_____

_____

TOWARD THE PROVERBIAL
PURPOSE IN LIFE

*I*n many cultures, there are long-held beliefs about one's purpose in life or the pursuit of one's purpose. A great many books have been written about it. There are movies and plays and essays and blogs—a seemingly endless stream of perspectives on purpose and the true meaning of life. Who among us hasn't hungered, at least once, to feel that our existence has value beyond the mundane things we say and do on a daily basis?

- Who am I?
- Why am I here?
- What was I meant to do?
- Who am I meant to be?

We have come to believe that purpose is one of the defining characteristics of being human. Purpose is the thing that gets you out of the house and across town on a cold snowy day for an activity that you won't be compensated for. It is what makes you smile when all of your energy is spent. Without purpose, there's often a severe price to be paid.

My tumble to the bottom was exacerbated when I lost my sense of purpose and my return to the mainstream was accelerated when I connected with a sense of purpose. Luckily, as human beings, we are resourceful with as many ways of finding purpose as there are potential purposes to be found. Every scenario, every event or occurrence, every context or condition, every idea can hold a rich sense of purpose depending on how you look at it.

But people in the struggle to find the ONE thing that they were meant to do—the ONE thing they were meant to be— sometimes find themselves at a loss. There's the experience of something being missing from life. There's the experience of being unfulfilled or empty. But why?

It is due to the "one purpose syndrome." The notion that each of us was meant for only one thing is a pretty limiting proposition. The one purpose syndrome, for a great many people, inevitably leads to disappointment and frustration because little else is possible when you have only one purpose.

But what if human beings are really "purpose-fluid?" What if, instead of having one purpose, we can have many? What if we were meant to move from purpose to purpose to purpose, instead of landing on just one? Sometimes you can choose a purpose like being in service to others, which is so expansive that it allows you to do an infinite number of things within it.

AMAZING DAY MAKER 6: Follow your heart, and you'll experience the unfolding of your purpose again and again and again.

<u>Pillar Two</u>
MY AMAZING DAY-MAKER JOURNAL

Day 36: What is your purpose?

_____

_____

_____

_____

_____

_____

_____

_____

_____

_____

_____

_____

_____

_____

_____

_____

_____

_____

<u>Pillar Two</u>

MY AMAZING DAY-MAKER JOURNAL

Day 37: A "purpose-fluid" life is generative, constantly evolving and creating anew. How does that apply to your life (past, present, or future) and your purpose?

_____

_____

_____

_____

_____

_____

_____

_____

_____

_____

_____

_____

_____

_____

Pillar Two

MY AMAZING DAY-MAKER JOURNAL

Day 38: What are the driving forces behind your purpose(s)? Were you born into it as part of your family lineage? Was there someone who inspired you toward your purpose? Did something happen to reveal your purpose to you?

_____

_____

_____

_____

_____

_____

_____

_____

_____

_____

_____

_____

_____

_____

Pillar Two
MY AMAZING DAY-MAKER JOURNAL

Day 39: When you are "living on purpose," what happens? What are you doing that works? What are you experiencing because of it?

_____

_____

_____

_____

_____

_____

_____

_____

_____

_____

_____

_____

_____

_____

_____

Pillar Two
MY AMAZING DAY-MAKER JOURNAL

Day 40: What talents or gifts have you discovered about yourself in the fulfillment of your purpose? What have you done that you didn't know you could do? What new ideas have been sparked by your purpose?

_____

_____

_____

_____

_____

_____

_____

_____

_____

_____

_____

_____

_____

_____

_____

Pillar Two

MY AMAZING DAY-MAKER JOURNAL

Day 41: Read what you wrote on Days 36, 37, 38, 39, and 40. Write your purpose statement beginning with the words I AM.

_____

_____

_____

_____

_____

_____

_____

_____

_____

_____

_____

_____

_____

_____

<u>Pillar Two</u>

MY AMAZING DAY-MAKER JOURNAL

Day 42: You are an amazing day maker. What possibility will you create today that will have you "living on purpose?"

_____

_____

_____

_____

_____

_____

_____

_____

_____

_____

_____

_____

_____

_____

LIVING IN THE LIGHT

*S*elf-awareness is an important facet of the Expansion Principle. It results from taking an honest, unvarnished look at your life without any attachment to the findings being right or wrong, good or bad.

- How well do you know yourself?
- How deeply do you understand your motivations?
- What drives you?
- Are you motivated by your own self-image?
- Or is how others experience you the driving force for your motivation?

Like having a sense of purpose, the importance of knowing oneself is a centuries-old belief that has never been more relevant than it is today. Psychologist Daniel Goleman has conducted research showing that self-awareness is essential to both goal setting and achievement. It helps shape emotional intelligence in a way that gives you an advantage when the circumstantial odds may not be in your favor.

How can you build self-awareness? You lay the foundation by understanding your "narrative identity" or the stories you tell yourself about your life.

Research indicates that narrative identity not only

shapes our personalities, it *becomes* our personalities. How you understand your narrative frames your current actions and future goals, not to mention your potential for achieving those goals. It's another example of how thoughts become things.

You can also grow in self-awareness by making self-reflection a daily practice. Whenever I take twenty minutes or so to reflect on my life and the things that matter most, it's as if I can feel the changes occurring in my brain. It's a kind of mindfulness that induces confidence, calm, and well-being.

And if you're really serious about growing in self-awareness, seek feedback. Seek feedback consistently.

We all have traits that others see in us but we don't see them in ourselves. They're called blind spots, and everyone has them. Feedback illuminates the blind spots and lets you know whether you are off the mark or right on target.

Expansion is improbable without growth in self-awareness and self-awareness is the active ingredient in the transformative process generally labeled as change.

AMAZING DAY MAKER 7: Trust yourself deeply as you uncover new facets of who you are.

<u>Pillar Two</u>

MY AMAZING DAY-MAKER JOURNAL

Day 43: Think of a time in your life when you were sufficiently relaxed to say what you really felt, and to take your best shot at life. What was that like?

_____

_____

_____

_____

_____

_____

_____

_____

_____

_____

_____

_____

_____

_____

_____

_____

<u>Pillar Two</u>

MY AMAZING DAY-MAKER JOURNAL

Day 44: Read Day 43's question and your response. What if the occasion you described was an example of you trusting yourself? What would trusting yourself look like now? What would trusting yourself reveal now?

_____

_____

_____

_____

_____

_____

_____

_____

_____

_____

_____

_____

_____

_____

_____

_____

<u>Pillar Two</u>

MY AMAZING DAY-MAKER JOURNAL

Day 45: Entertainment mogul and megastar Beyoncé once said, "I don't like to gamble. But if there's one thing I'm willing to bet on, it's myself." Think of a time when you bet on yourself, a time when you could be your whole self. What was that like?

_____

_____

_____

_____

_____

_____

_____

_____

_____

_____

_____

_____

_____

_____

Pillar Two
MY AMAZING DAY-MAKER JOURNAL

Day 46: You are whole and complete as you are. What does that mean to you?

_____

_____

_____

_____

_____

_____

_____

_____

_____

_____

_____

_____

_____

_____

Pillar Two
MY AMAZING DAY-MAKER JOURNAL

Day 47: Read what you wrote on Days 43, 44, 45, and 46. Circle some of the words and phrases that stand out or move you in some way. Using those words and phrases, write an I AM statement(s) affirming the trust you have in yourself.

_____

_____

_____

_____

_____

_____

_____

_____

_____

_____

_____

_____

_____

Pillar Two
MY AMAZING DAY-MAKER JOURNAL

Day 48: You are an amazing day maker. How will you use that skill in the service of others today?

_____

_____

_____

_____

_____

_____

_____

_____

_____

_____

_____

_____

_____

_____

_____

_____

<u>Pillar Two</u>
MY AMAZING DAY-MAKER JOURNAL

Day 49: Complete the following two statements in as much detail as possible. I am eager to be in service to _____ Because of it, I see these possibilities:

_____

_____

_____

_____

_____

_____

_____

_____

_____

_____

_____

_____

_____

_____

_____

EMERGENCE

Choosing To Move Forward.
Choosing To Move Upward.

YOU ARE MORE RESILIENT
THAN YOU KNOW

*R*esilience allows you, me, or anyone else to come back stronger than ever after seemingly being pummeled by life itself. Resilience is about overcoming. It is about human resolve and the ability to "rise from the ashes." Resilient people see failure and setbacks as forms of feedback that empower them to change course and soldier on.

The first time I looked back on how I was able to rebuild my life, one revelation was that I was far more resilient than I could have imagined. I had never even thought about resilience and how to apply it in a determined and focused manner until then. I had lived my life at the fringes of human existence for a period that seems like a thousand torturous years condensed into a blink of an eye. Yet I was able to emerge. I was able to not only bounce back, but to bounce forward as well.

It is in bouncing forward that I was empowered to write this book and to not only live my dream life, but my best life, as well.

How resilient are you? Regardless of your answer, you are exponentially more resilient than you think you are and you will succeed in ways you probably cannot even imagine. Resilience is the lifeblood of Emergence.

In Emergence you'll ask questions such as:

Who am I?

What do I believe?

How should I live my life?

To examine these questions thoroughly, it is important to hold the belief that resilience is possible, come what may, and that you are more resilient than you think. Blessed with a positive attitude, optimism, authenticity, and the ability to see failure as feedback, resilient people always find a way to create anew.

AMAZING DAY MAKER 8: If you quote Dr. Seuss over and over today, something extraordinary may come your way.

> *"Today you are You. That is truer than true.*
> *There is no one alive who is Youer than You."*
> –Dr. Seuss

<u>Pillar Three</u>

MY AMAZING DAY-MAKER JOURNAL

Day 50: Write a poem or limerick that is either about you or to you.

_____

_____

_____

_____

_____

_____

_____

_____

_____

_____

_____

_____

_____

_____

<u>Pillar Three</u>

MY AMAZING DAY-MAKER JOURNAL

Day 51: Think of a time when you felt life had knocked you down. How did you feel about being knocked down? What made you rise again?

_____

_____

_____

_____

_____

_____

_____

_____

_____

_____

_____

_____

_____

_____

_____

Pillar Three
MY AMAZING DAY-MAKER JOURNAL

Day 52: Realizing the answer is ever-evolving, what right now is the best life you see possible for yourself?

_____

_____

_____

_____

_____

_____

_____

_____

_____

_____

_____

_____

_____

_____

_____

_____

<u>Pillar Three</u>

MY AMAZING DAY-MAKER JOURNAL

Day 53: Who are you?

_____

_____

_____

_____

_____

_____

_____

_____

_____

_____

_____

_____

_____

_____

_____

_____

_____

Pillar Three
MY AMAZING DAY-MAKER JOURNAL

Day 54: Identify and describe at least four core beliefs by which you live your life.

1.

_____

_____

_____

2.

_____

_____

_____

3.

_____

_____

_____

4.

_____

_____

_____

Pillar Three
MY AMAZING DAY-MAKER JOURNAL

Day 55: To grow yourself in resiliency, be sure to incorporate these statements into your belief system (if they're not there already). Place your attention on them today and every day:

- I have powerful relationships, a supportive structure, strong role models, and plenty of evidence that says I matter.
- I am a person who has hope and faith, cares about others, is proud of herself/himself, and has a possibility mindset.
- I can communicate effectively, solve problems, motivate myself, and inspire others.

<u>Pillar Three</u>
MY AMAZING DAY-MAKER JOURNAL

Day 56: You're an amazing day maker. What amazingness will you create today?

_____

_____

_____

_____

_____

_____

_____

_____

_____

_____

_____

_____

_____

_____

THE FLAWLESSNESS MESS

"Perfection is the enemy of greatness."
–Janelle Monae

*W*hat a powerful statement. In psychology it's called perfectionism, a personality trait characterized by a person's striving for flawlessness and the setting of high-performance standards. None of this is inherently adverse, of course, but add to it critical self-evaluations and concerns regarding others' evaluations, and perfectionism can become a narrow, frustrating and unfulfilling practice that can have the opposite of the desired impact. I call it the flawlessness mess. It's a bit like treading water, there's a lot of motion going on, but you're not really going anywhere.

Michelangelo, the Italian sculptor, painter, architect, and poet of the High Renaissance period said, "The true work of art is but a shadow of the divine perfection."

You are a perfectly imperfect divine work of art and in the quest for perfection, a great work of art can be misjudged or overlooked. When I was at the depths of my despair, perfectionism kept me down. The constant comparisons to ill-founded ideals, sometimes my own and sometimes others', meant I couldn't quite get my footing. I couldn't create a suitable foundation on which to build my goals, dreams, and vision. Perfectionism consumed my time and attention, yielding little along the way.

It was when I started looking at my everyday habits, with the goal of changing nonproductive thoughts and behaviors that often led to negative outcomes, that I was able to escape the grip of perfectionism. Looking back, I now see that I started developing life-affirming ways to think and behave. With conscious awareness and a daily focus on changing old habits, I was able to build new, positive emotional experiences.

Experts say our brains possess the capacity for neuroplasticity. Meaning, practicing new ways of thinking and behaving can actually change our brain neurons and the pathways between them. It's important to have a mindset that allows for flexibility. Perfectionism can result from a rigid mindset in which you don't change your expectations based on the situation.

Second-guessing, procrastinating, always feeling overwhelmed, feeling like an imposter, or giving up and not trying are all indicators of a tendency toward perfectionism. To combat perfectionism, I had to remove the "shoulds" and give myself credit for trying. I stopped believing every mistake was a disaster and I learned to structure my goals within a realistic timeframe. Details matter, but so does the bigger picture and I found tremendous freedom in the belief that perfection, as an ideal, allows for the creation of excellence along the way to achieving it.

> *"My mother was extremely controlled, sort of*
> *flawless. And I always tend to be a bit more*
> *hippie."* –Vera Wang

AMAZING DAY MAKER 9: Be more hippie today.

Pillar Three
MY AMAZING DAY-MAKER JOURNAL

Day 57: Regardless of how much of a hippie you are already, what would it mean for you to be more hippie? What would be different? What would you accomplish? How would you feel?

_____

_____

_____

_____

_____

_____

_____

_____

_____

_____

_____

_____

_____

_____

Pillar Three
MY AMAZING DAY-MAKER JOURNAL

Day 58: Read what you wrote on Day 57. Assuming you were more hippie yesterday, what has the experience taught you? If you weren't more hippie yesterday, be more hippie today and then respond to Day 58's original question.

_____

_____

_____

_____

_____

_____

_____

_____

_____

_____

_____

_____

_____

_____

_____

_____

<u>Pillar Three</u>
MY AMAZING DAY-MAKER JOURNAL

Day 59: Practice a new way of thinking today. If you're the type who rarely seeks advice, get someone's advice on something today. If you're the type who does in-depth research before reaching a conclusion, make snap decisions today. Whatever is a departure from how you normally think, do that. Begin by describing it here:

_____

_____

_____

_____

_____

_____

_____

_____

_____

_____

_____

_____

_____

_____

Pillar Three
MY AMAZING DAY-MAKER JOURNAL

Day 60: Think of something you've been putting off. Maybe a household chore or task. Maybe it's something at work. Maybe it's a difficult conversation. Whatever it is, act on it today. Begin by declaring it here. What will it be?

_____

_____

_____

_____

_____

_____

_____

_____

_____

_____

_____

_____

_____

Pillar Three
MY AMAZING DAY-MAKER JOURNAL

Day 61: Tap into your thoughts. Spend time with those that you sense are life-affirming. Are they thoughts about your family? Are they thoughts about your future or your past? Are your life-affirming thoughts about you?

_____

_____

_____

_____

_____

_____

_____

_____

_____

_____

_____

_____

_____

_____

Pillar Three
MY AMAZING DAY-MAKER JOURNAL

Day 62: What do you find most compelling about yourself? Is it your zest for life? Is it your tenacity or focus? What makes your engine roar?

_____

_____

_____

_____

_____

_____

_____

_____

_____

_____

_____

_____

_____

_____

Pillar Three
MY AMAZING DAY-MAKER JOURNAL

Day 63: Read your entries on Days 57 - 62. Taken altogether, what do you think this says about you? What does it say to you?

_____

_____

_____

_____

_____

_____

_____

_____

_____

_____

_____

_____

_____

_____

IT'S IMPORTANT WHO YOU KNOW

*H*ealth researchers say chronic negative emotions can influence emotional and mental health, along with physical well-being. That's one reason why it's important to choose your relationships carefully. It's important who you know and whose company you keep. Sometimes you need somebody to believe in you until you can believe in yourself.

My dear friend and mentor, Robin Diane Lynn, was the one who believed in me and taught me the importance of believing in myself. In many ways, she was the queen of the tribe that I claimed as my own in the rebuilding of my life. Having strong, positive social support, is one of the most important factors in predicting the physical health and well-being in people of all ages. Support and encouragement can even be effective at relieving stress.

Had Robin not been my devoted cheerleader shouting "yes you can" in response to my "I can't" time and time again, I would not be having this conversation with you about the pillars of amazingness. Robin taught me that I need not be crushed by the weight of my past and that it's important to surround myself with people who have a possibility mindset and aren't afraid to show it. She impressed upon me that powerful people live purposeful lives. The only thing I knew Robin to ever succumb to was pancreatic cancer and yet she continues to have an impact on people around the world because she empowered so many others.

But be careful not to confuse positive support with being around happy people. I love being around happy people but I'm talking about surrounding yourself with people who support you in your goals, encourage you, and help you feel good about yourself. As an amazing day maker, you can actually cultivate this kind of support in your existing relationships as well as in new ones.

AMAZING DAY MAKER 10: Find someone who could use a cheerleader; then shake your pompoms for their success!

MY AMAZING DAY-MAKER JOURNAL

Day 64: Think about the people you spend the most time with and make a narrative list of them. Reflect on your typical experiences with them. Who are they? What is it like to be around them?

_____

_____

_____

_____

_____

_____

_____

_____

_____

_____

_____

_____

_____

_____

_____

_____

Pillar Three
MY AMAZING DAY-MAKER JOURNAL

Day 65: Read what you wrote on Day 64. From that list, select the people around whom you feel refreshed, those who generate a sense of excitement, and people around whom you feel accepted and heard. Reflect on them. Write about them.

_____

_____

_____

_____

_____

_____

_____

_____

_____

_____

_____

_____

_____

<u>Pillar Three</u>

MY AMAZING DAY-MAKER JOURNAL

Day 66: Read what you wrote on Day 65. Circle the words or attributes that stand out or that move you in some way. Write them down and discuss why these attributes are important to you.

_____

_____

_____

_____

_____

_____

_____

_____

_____

_____

_____

_____

_____

_____

Pillar Three
MY AMAZING DAY-MAKER JOURNAL

Day 67: Read the list of people on Day 65 again. These are people who empower you. Spending time with them and others like them can positively impact the achievement of your goals, dreams, and vision. What do you see as possible because of your relationship with them?

_____

_____

_____

_____

_____

_____

_____

_____

_____

_____

_____

_____

_____

_____

<u>Pillar Three</u>

MY AMAZING DAY-MAKER JOURNAL

Day 68: Assuming "You get what you give," how will you be someone's cheerleader today? What encouragement will you offer? Whose life will be forwarded by you today, and what will you do or say to forward that person?

_____

_____

_____

_____

_____

_____

_____

_____

_____

_____

_____

_____

_____

_____

Pillar Three
MY AMAZING DAY-MAKER JOURNAL

Day 69: Review your journal entries for Days 64 – 68. What kind of people empower you? What do they say to you? What do you think they say about you when you're not with them?

_____

_____

_____

_____

_____

_____

_____

_____

_____

_____

_____

_____

_____

_____

Pillar Three

MY AMAZING DAY-MAKER JOURNAL

Day 70: You're an amazing day-maker. What evidence is there that proves that? What amazingness can the world count on from you today?

_____

_____

_____

_____

_____

_____

_____

_____

_____

_____

_____

_____

_____

_____

LET'S HEAR IT FOR THE JANITOR!

here's a lot to admire about former First Lady Michelle Obama. She's a trailblazer with a long list of firsts to her credit. She's smart, witty, powerful, compassionate, and she looks great in everything she wears. She's also a woman of service and contribution who recognizes the role that others have played in her success. Equally important, she appreciates the role that she can play in the empowerment of others.

"We learned about gratitude and humility—that so many people had a hand in our success," Mrs. Obama said in a speech, *"From the teachers who inspired us to the janitors who kept our school clean... and we were taught to value everyone's contribution and treat everyone with respect."*

I was profoundly moved by those words and they continue to resonate with me every time I read them. A great many people have had a hand in the rebuilding of my life. Earlier, I told you about Robin, my mentor and friend, who believed in me even when I didn't believe in myself. She also modeled what it means to take a stand for people and that has become the underpinning of the path that I'm on...this ever-unfolding journey of self-discovery, service and contribution, and pure possibility.

I never have to look too far or too long to touch the

hand of someone who has inspired me or contributed to my life in some way. From the unidentified commuter train conductor who helped shape my outlook each day by the way she joyfully announced every stop and invited exiting passengers to "step lively" to the fashion executive who taught me to navigate my way in the corporate world to family and friends who share themselves so freely. I am the sum total of their contribution to me. And in turn, I am able to contribute to others. Author Melody Beattie said, "Gratitude unlocks the fullness of life. It turns what we have into enough, and more. It turns denial into acceptance, chaos to order, confusion to clarity. It can turn a meal into a feast, a house into a home, a stranger into a friend."

So, let's hear it for the janitor! Shout out to the homeroom teacher! Kudos to the cashier at the drugstore! Bravo to the unrelenting friend! And yay you!

AMAZING DAY MAKER 11: Be grateful. Be grateful for everyone. Be grateful for everything. Act grateful. And in all matters, give thanks.

Pillar Three
MY AMAZING DAY-MAKER JOURNAL

Day 71: What does it mean to be grateful? When you're grateful, what sorts of things do you do? What kinds of things do you say?

_____

_____

_____

_____

_____

_____

_____

_____

_____

_____

_____

_____

_____

_____

_____

Pillar Three
MY AMAZING DAY-MAKER JOURNAL

Day 72: Take a look at your smartphone or just bring it to mind. What wireless carrier provides your service? Approximately how many apps are on it? How many songs by how many musicians are on it? Your smartphone makes life easier. What would it mean to thank EVERYONE who had a hand in making your life easier by manufacturing, distributing, or servicing your smartphone? What would it mean to do this for everything that makes your life easier and everything that does not?

_____

_____

_____

_____

_____

_____

_____

_____

_____

_____

_____

Pillar Three
MY AMAZING DAY-MAKER JOURNAL

Day 73: Make a list of people for whom you're grateful because they impacted your life in a positive way. State specifically why you're grateful for each person on your list.

_____

_____

_____

_____

_____

_____

_____

_____

_____

_____

_____

_____

_____

_____

<u>Pillar Three</u>

MY AMAZING DAY-MAKER JOURNAL

Day 74: Imagine that there are other people in the world creating gratitude lists like the one that you created yesterday. Whose list would you be on, and what would each person be grateful to you for?

_____

_____

_____

_____

_____

_____

_____

_____

_____

_____

_____

_____

_____

_____

_____

Pillar Three
MY AMAZING DAY-MAKER JOURNAL

Day 75: You are an amazing day maker. How will you use that gift to further your vision of what it means to live a life of gratitude today?

_____

_____

_____

_____

_____

_____

_____

_____

_____

_____

_____

_____

_____

_____

<u>Pillar Three</u>
MY AMAZING DAY-MAKER JOURNAL

Day 76: What are you most looking forward to in the everyday practice of gratitude?

_____

_____

_____

_____

_____

_____

_____

_____

_____

_____

_____

_____

_____

_____

_____

Pillar Three
MY AMAZING DAY-MAKER JOURNAL

Day 77: Write your personal gratitude statement as a broad description of what gratitude looks like for you. Begin with I AM:

_____

_____

_____

_____

_____

_____

_____

_____

_____

_____

_____

_____

_____

_____

THE INCENDIARY NATURE
OF INTENTION

*A*nother key aspect of Emergence is the practice of setting clear intentions. But what is intention? It is the spark that ignites your power to create. It is the thought that leads to the declaration that leads to the actions that lead to the tangible manifestation of your goal or vision.

Intention usually leans toward things such as relationships, love, self-improvement, attitude or outlook, and career. Intention also is meant to affect our emotional, physical, or psychological selves in the process of reaching the goal. It's a positive call to action about something you're committed to doing, rather than something you do not want to do, but feel that you "should."

When setting intention, it is important to do so in a focused manner within a chosen structure, which can be a ritual of your own design. Every year on New Year's Eve, a friend of mine makes a list of the goals and dreams she is committed to manifesting in the year ahead. She also writes down how she wants to feel in the process of creating each item on the list. That's the structure she's chosen for certain intentions. You, on the other hand, might prefer to sit by the window with a cup of your favorite tea and a sketch pad to illustrate your intentions. The idea is that you not allow your intentions to be random. Make sure they're focused and within a structure that leaves you feeling inspired and uplifted.

Be specific when distilling your intentions. Similar to the old computer programing maxim, "garbage in, garbage out." If you start with an ineffective or disempowering thought, what you reap will be ineffective and disempowering. So, dive into the beautiful details of your goal and describe the experience of achieving it, not just at the end, but along the way as well.

Be creative with your intention and allow for an abundance of next-level inspiration. Some examples of intention may be to practice mindfulness, achieve inner peace, make spiritual connections, initiate cleansing, stretch daily, work out regularly, celebrate life joyously, relax more often, learn a new skill, grow in self-awareness, practice self-care, etc.

This is probably a good time to remind you that what may seem impossible now will someday be a valuable theme in the retelling of how you made it happen. I know this from my own experience. The published book you are currently reading, seemed impossible only eighteen months ago. Yet, I set my intention and now *It's a Great Day to be Amazing!*

Trust God by believing in yourself. Trust God by being flexible within the demands of life. Take committed actions toward your goal.

"You are what your deepest desire is. As your desire is, so is your intention. As your intention is, so is your will. As your will is, so is your deed. As your deed is, so is your destiny."
–From the Upanishads, Vedic Sacred Text

AMAZING DAY MAKER 12: Dream big.

Pillar Three
MY AMAZING DAY-MAKER JOURNAL

Day 78: Make a narrative list of some of your intentions. Begin with, **My intention is:**

_____

_____

_____

_____

_____

_____

_____

_____

_____

_____

_____

_____

_____

_____

_____

_____

_____

Pillar Three

MY AMAZING DAY-MAKER JOURNAL

Day 79: Make a list of what you intend to do or accomplish. Be specific. Use empowering words and thoughts that make you feel good or inspire you in some way. Avoid words such as "should," "always," "must," or "never."

_____

_____

_____

_____

_____

_____

_____

_____

_____

_____

_____

_____

_____

_____

<u>Pillar Three</u>

MY AMAZING DAY-MAKER JOURNAL

Day 80: Read what you wrote on Day 78. Say your intentions out loud as you rewrite them on these pages. Also, say them out loud or to yourself throughout the course of the day.

_____

_____

_____

_____

_____

_____

_____

_____

_____

_____

_____

_____

_____

_____

_____

<u>Pillar Three</u>
MY AMAZING DAY-MAKER JOURNAL

Day 81: Read what you wrote on Day 79. Rewrite the list of what you intend to do or accomplish. Be specific. Tweak if necessary.

_____

_____

_____

_____

_____

_____

_____

_____

_____

_____

_____

_____

_____

_____

Pillar Three
MY AMAZING DAY-MAKER JOURNAL

Day 82: What will you do today to show your commitment to one of your intentions? For example, if you want to begin to practice mindfulness, listen to two or more mindfulness meditations today.

_____

_____

_____

_____

_____

_____

_____

_____

_____

_____

_____

_____

_____

_____

Pillar Three

MY AMAZING DAY-MAKER JOURNAL

Day 83: To deepen your commitment, share your intention with others today. Start by jotting down a few things about what you will say and to whom.

_____

_____

_____

_____

_____

_____

_____

_____

_____

_____

_____

_____

_____

_____

_____

Pillar Three
MY AMAZING DAY-MAKER JOURNAL

Day 84: It's a great day to be amazing. Why is that?

_____

_____

_____

_____

_____

_____

_____

_____

_____

_____

_____

_____

_____

_____

_____

_____

FAILURE ISN'T FATAL WHEN
YOU HAVE COURAGE

*I*n everything from history books to fairytales, and myths to movies, courage is depicted as an attribute of character involving self-sacrifice for the greater good. Those of us in Western Culture, for example, were given a steady diet of heroic and inspirational stories that were often far removed from our own everyday lives. Courage is often portrayed as something to aspire to, as opposed to something innate in everyone. What if courage is personal, and therefore self-defined?

I know someone who gave away most of her possessions and moved from New York City to a mountain village in eSwatini where she lives in a hut and works with village youth. To me, that takes courage. But to my friend who is doing it, there's nothing courageous about it.

There are different types of courage, ranging from physical strength and endurance to mental stamina and innovation. What's courage to you?

Sometimes courage is feeling fear and choosing to act in the face of it. Sometimes it's following your heart and daring to pursue your dreams or persevering in the face of adversity. There are times when courage is standing for what is just and right and having the willingness to be responsible for everything.

What is courage to you? Be courageous by your own design.

AMAZING DAY MAKER BONUS: Take a leap of faith.

<u>Pillar Three</u>

MY AMAZING DAY-MAKER JOURNAL

Day 85: What is courage to you?

_____

_____

_____

_____

_____

_____

_____

_____

_____

_____

_____

_____

_____

_____

_____

_____

_____

<u>Pillar Three</u>
MY AMAZING DAY-MAKER JOURNAL

Day 86: Think of a time when you were courageous. Describe the situation you faced and the courageous action you took.

_____

_____

_____

_____

_____

_____

_____

_____

_____

_____

_____

_____

_____

_____

_____

Pillar Three

MY AMAZING DAY-MAKER JOURNAL

Day 87: Read what you wrote on Days 85 and 86. Looking toward the future, what courageous acts will be required of you in the fulfillment of your goals?

_____

_____

_____

_____

_____

_____

_____

_____

_____

_____

_____

_____

_____

_____

_____

_____

<u>Pillar Three</u>

MY AMAZING DAY-MAKER JOURNAL

Day 88: Think of something you've been avoiding for a very long time. Describe what it is as well as the actions you'll take today to no longer avoid it.

_____

_____

_____

_____

_____

_____

_____

_____

_____

_____

_____

_____

_____

_____

_____

<u>Pillar Three</u>
MY AMAZING DAY-MAKER JOURNAL

Day 89: Read what you wrote on Day 88. Now think of something ELSE that you've been avoiding for a very long time. Describe what it is as well as the actions you'll take today to no longer avoid it.

_____

_____

_____

_____

_____

_____

_____

_____

_____

_____

_____

_____

_____

<u>Pillar Three</u>

MY AMAZING DAY-MAKER JOURNAL

Day 90: Don't go it alone. There is courage in numbers. Think about the people who empower you. Let's call them your Courage Crew. Who are they and what's great about them?

_____

_____

_____

_____

_____

_____

_____

_____

_____

_____

_____

_____

_____

_____

<u>Pillar Three</u>
MY AMAZING DAY-MAKER JOURNAL

Day 91: You've made some powerful declarations over the last 90 days. Declarations about who you are and what you stand for, as well as what you're committed to. These declarations originate from the soul. Write down your thoughts about that.

_____

_____

_____

_____

_____

_____

_____

_____

_____

_____

_____

_____

_____

THE BEGINNING

*T*hank you and congratulations on stepping into ***Possibilitology***! You now have a structure for the practice of possibility thinking (PT).

I encourage you to return to ***Possibilitology: It's a Great Day to be Amazing*** again and again and to reread the principles, the *Amazing Day-Makers*, and your journal entries. Over time, your responses to the prompts may change. That's simply evidence of your growth, your ever-widening perspective, and of the strengthening of your ability to effectively address life's challenges as well as life's opportunities.

My team and I have created a number of resources to support and empower you in the practice of possibility thinking through *Possibilitology*. Put the maximum impact of PT to work in your life by enrolling in one of our in-person workshops or eLearning courses. Subscribe to our newsletter. Travel to an exotic destination with us to make a difference on one of our purpose-centered tours. Maybe you would like to add *Possibilitology* apparel to your wardrobe, or surround yourself with all of the inspiring, forward-moving, upward moving messaging that *Possibilitology* has to offer.

Since "possibility loves company," invite your family members and friends to help you make every day an amazing day!

With Love,

Vallori Thomas

www.ValloriThomas.com

SPECIAL ACKNOWLEDGMENTS

*A sincere thank you to all the Possibilitarians
who inspired me and stood with me as we
brought to life the principles and practices to
have each and every day be AMAZING!*

Lesley Beckwith, Raimana Cowan, Lena Koropey, Tariq Franklin, Adreina Adams, Samantha Wonder, Alexus Ruiz, Myra Brevard, Akilah Thompson, Pooran Rambaran, Natacha Jospitre, Jamila LaMont, Dilenia Frias, Flo Washington, Keisha Knowles Phelps, Shawn Verdee, Tawana Richards, Pauline Gayle, Ineisha Williford, Teresa Green, Colleen Edwards, Nicole White, Roma Koropey, Sharon Addison, Robert Hoagland, Melitsa Davis, Norva Alleyne, Taundrea Tavada, Roberto Ventura, Esther Pressler, Fabiola Lesperance, Royalty Lee, Demarcus McGaughey, Krystal Figaro, Andy Hutchinson, Derrick Johnson, Eliza Raymond, Shelley Bragg, Tyquane Bates.

My Courage Crew

Demarcus McGaughey, my ROD ATWU, thank you for being such an artful influence in my life. Curtis Dennis, thank you for giving wings to so many of my ideas. Sylvia High, aka Phenomenal Woman, I'm grateful that Aiming High is not just the name of your company, but how you elevate others.

Vivian Anderson Patterson, kudos to you for your amazing strength and giving heart. Finally, thank you, Mynd Matters Publishing, for your partnership.